THIS BOOK BELONGS TO

_____

YOU ARE PRICELESS

THE PARABLE OF THE BICYCLE

For Katharine

—*Stephen Robinson*

For Daddy's little girls, Cindy, Sarah, and Anna Marie

—*Ben Sowards*

Visit us at shadowmountain.com

ISBN 1-59038-361-3

Printed in China   70582
Phoenix Asia

10   9   8   7   6   5   4   3   2   1

YOU ARE PRICELESS

The Parable of the Bicycle

Written by Stephen E. Robinson ✦ Illustrated by Ben Sowards

SHADOW
MOUNTAIN

"Daddy, I need to talk to you," the little girl said. Seeing her earnest expression, the father set his newspaper aside and looked into his daughter's eyes.

"All my friends have bikes," the little girl explained. "Can I get a bike? I could ride it to school and lock it with a lock. I could go to my friend's house all by myself and you wouldn't even have to drive me." Her eyes sparkled with excitement at the thought.

W ell," he said, "that is an interesting idea. But having a bike is a big responsibility, you know. And bikes cost quite a lot of money."

The little girl smiled confidently. "I'm going to pay for it myself," she declared. "I'm going to save up all my money and not spend even one penny. If I save and save, don't you think I'll have enough for a bike someday?"

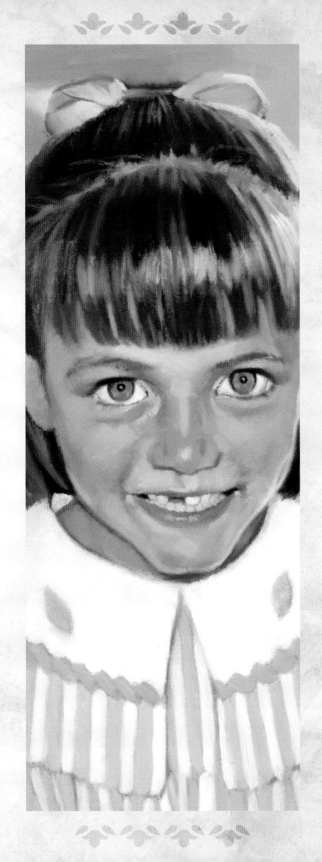

T he father sat for a few moments without answering.

He knew that his little girl had no idea what a bicycle

would really cost. There was no way her small allowance

would be enough, even if she did extra jobs around the

house to add to it.

But she was so excited, so earnest—so priceless—that

his heart melted. He took her into his arms and hugged

her tightly. "A goal is a good thing to have," he said.

"Why don't you try it, and let's see what happens."

A few days went by, and the father found his little girl sweeping the porch. The following week he noticed her working alongside her mother in the garden, pulling weeds and planting flowers. And once or twice, as the little girl went into her bedroom, he heard the clink of coins being dropped into a glass jar.

After a while, the little girl came to her father and said, "Daddy, I've been working and saving up all my money for a long time. Can we get my bike now?" She shook the coins in the bottom of the jar.

The father looked at the little collection of coins, and then he looked into the pleading eyes of the little girl he loved so much. "Let's go and see what we can find out," he suggested.

The bicycle shop had a little bell that made a tinkling noise when they walked into the store. They hadn't looked around very long when suddenly the little girl froze. There it was! The most beautiful bicycle she could ever have imagined! She ran to it, stroking its shiny chrome and running her fingers through the colorful streamers that flowed from its handle grips. Never could there be a more perfect bike than this one. She clapped her hands with the pure delight of it. ᴓ

Then she reached for the price tag.

The next moment, the sunshine in the little girl's eyes melted into tears. "Oh, Daddy," she wept, "I'll never have enough. Never." She threw herself into his arms.

Her father cradled her head on his shoulder and gently stroked her hair, letting her cry. ∽

When the little girl finally settled down, her father wiped her tears away and said, "How about this? How much money *do* you have?"

"Sixty-one cents," she answered in a forlorn voice.

"Then I'll tell you what," he said. "Let's try a different arrangement. You give me everything you've got—the whole sixty-one cents—and a hug and a kiss, and this bike is yours. I'll make up the difference."

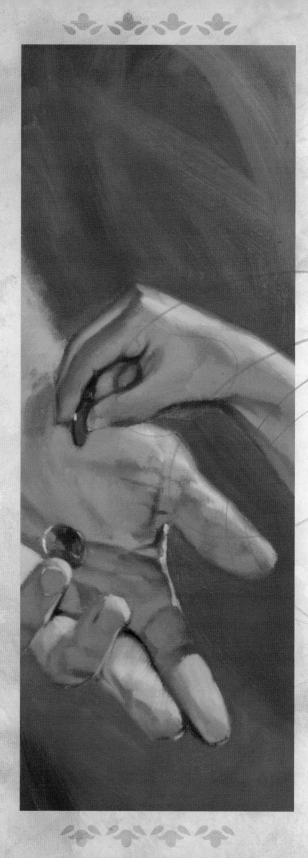

Hope came back into the little girl's eyes. "Really, Daddy?" she asked.

"Really, honey."

"Oh, Daddy!" she said once again, but the words were happy ones now, and the little girl hurried to fill her part of the bargain with several hugs and kisses just to be sure. ∾

The deal was completed, and the Most Perfect Bike Ever was purchased, and the father walked beside his little girl as she wheeled it proudly to the car. In his pockets jingled the sixty-one cents, and in his heart glowed his love for his daughter and the joy he felt in knowing how hard she had worked to reach her goal. When it came down to it, the sixty-one cents—and the hugs and kisses—were exactly enough.

But the story doesn't end there. . . .

The truth is, there's something we all want, and we want it more than any child ever wanted any bicycle. We want the kingdom of God. We want to go home to our Father in Heaven worthy and clean.

At some point in that spiritual voyage, we recognize the full price of admission into that kingdom, and we also realize we cannot pay it. We'll never have enough—never. The tremendous price of perfect performance is hopelessly beyond our means.

And so we despair.

Only then can we fully appreciate the One who comes to save. For Him, each soul is priceless. When we finally feel the pain of our own shortcomings, the Savior, Jesus Christ, steps in and lovingly says, "Let's try a different arrangement. How much *do* you have? You give me exactly that much (the whole sixty-one cents) and do all you *can* do, and I will provide the rest for now. You give me all you've got, and a hug and a kiss (signifying the love that cements this covenant), and the kingdom is yours. Perfection will still be our ultimate goal, but until you can achieve it on your own, I'll let you use mine. What do you say?"

To all who want to serve God and keep his commandments, who hunger and thirst after righteousness, we declare, *this* is the "good news" of the gospel. Christ is the answer. He is the bridge from here to there. He is our hope when we feel cut off and alone. He *is* our Savior.

"Ask, and it shall be given you; seek, and ye shall find; knock, and it shall be opened unto you: For every one that asketh receiveth; and he that seeketh findeth; and to him that knocketh it shall be opened."

— Matthew 7:7–8 —